Dedicated to My Mother

Prologue

It has been years since her body decayed, and became nothing but the earth again. Her soul vanishing to a world humans didn't quite understand, and many did not believe in. Children play above her on the grass and are scolded if they come close to her headstone. It has been years since my mother died, since she said goodbye to this world. It was ruled a natural death, something that just happened in her sleep, but I think my grandmother somehow managed to pay off the morgue and funeral home just to save face with all the neighbors.

I return to the house I once lived in, the walls still the same color, the furniture still in the same spot, with the same stains, and same smoke smell. My adult body somehow seems to shrink back to its childlike state when entering the house, but then returns to normal when it realizes it never truly was a child in this house, even at the early ages of six, eight, and ten. The cabinets contain the same things they always have: nothing. Staring out the window to the backyard and the rotten wooden deck, I realize something.

All those years of playing "hide and seek" just to see if my assumptions were true, I can do now without the cover up. Was it too childlike? Whatever I find won't change the situation, it won't bring her back to life, but a part of me won't be whole if I don't know, if I have the opportunity to find out, and don't seize it.

I start in her room, opening the creaky white paneled closet that sits back near the dead plant in the corner by the window. It still makes the same noise, and still gets caught in a specific place about 3/4ths the way open, and even after years of not being there, I still remember how to lift the knob a certain way to get it uncaught, and to put it back on track. Almost instantly, I go to the built in shelves that sit in the corner, digging through shoes, turning them upside down and shaking them a little too aggressively hoping something will fall out. Nothing.

I then go to the small entertainment center like piece of furniture that is against the back wall, opening the wicker baskets underneath, digging through looking for something. Nothing.

Through dismay, I pick myself off the ground, brushing off all the mix and match shit I found in the baskets, leaving them on the floor, for it doesn't matter if there is a mess or not, it blended in with the rest of the room anyway.

Out of curiosity, I wonder if my room was still there. I open the door with its many leftover tape pieces, from countless Tiger Beat posters that once hung all over it. The pink polka dotted walls still aligned with the white furniture, and my bright pink fuzzy chair still is in the corner, but this time without all the clothes. The room is spotless, definitely not like I had left it. She must have cleaned it every week, for years, in hopes I might return. I spin around, and close the door again softly as if not to disrupt anything.

I continue on my search, going back in the room, stepping over the mix and match things I left on the floor, into the bathroom, that had been remodeled countless times, but is somehow always out of date. I dig through the shit under the sink, and find it. All of it? I don't know, but a stash nonetheless. All sorts of drugs, under towels, in the back of plastic organizer drawers, hidden, but there. I cry. A soft tear, then knees weak, then on the floor crying. Why am I surprised?

I stare around at the pictures on the wall, at the green bed posts and yellow pillows, and see myself on days of "vegging out" which was an excuse for she had done too many drugs the day before, and needed to lay in bed. Those days were my favorite. We would eat food and watch reruns on tv. It was "girls only." Those days when her body was weak and her mind was gone, those were still my favorite though, because she was present. I walk into the hallway, holding the drugs, rubbing the powder around on my fingertips through the sealed bag, looking into the bathroom with the green tile and orange and yellow decorations. I can picture when I first got my period, and we had to call someone to bring us tampons because she had been drinking and couldn't drive. I imagine myself in the bathtub when she taught me to shave my legs, and I was scared her hands were too shaky, that she might cut me. I walk down the stairs, and imagine my brother when he walked around the corner of the dining room to the living room, with blood streaming down his face, crying "the dog did it to me," and I was the only one that could help. I imagine my stepfather sitting in the recliner, snoring, and I look back up the stairs to my mother's room, imagining her snoring too in the darkness of her room. I was the only one who could clean up the blood.

Anger began to come over me, my hands now shaking, my breath growing in intensity, tears pouring. I try to scream, but no words could come. I run into the kitchen, turning on the faucet, I will flush them out once and for all. Watch them as they dwindle to nothing under the water, in the sink as it swirls around and around the drain before falling to its death. Then I think about the time my brother flushed all his toy cars down the toilet and it clogged up everything in the backyard, and I remember how I had to talk to the construction workers when they came to fix it, because she was sleeping at three. My mind drifts and I think about what her mind thought, what her eyes saw, when she was under the influence of these drugs I held in my hand.

Before I could realize what I am doing, I start to shove them in my mouth, the powder all over my chin, the sink, in my mouth, swallowing. I allow my legs to cave, for my body to slide down the cabinets, embracing the cold floor and the stale kitchen mat. Within no time, it hits me. Faster than I thought, and I am scared.

A euphoria comes over me and the deep reds of the wall seem deeper, like my hair...so smooth...I love red. Why am I sweating? Who's playing the drum? Does anyone hear that, is anyone there? Hello? Why are these thoughts only in my head? My heartbeat. I think I am going to throw up. Fuck. Hello. Fuck. I call 911.

Soaked in sweat. These are nightmares I have often. They don't always go the same way, but they have the same idea. Overdose. Overdose. Overdose. Death. I guess it is true when they say, "You can close your eyes to reality, but not to memories." It just seems to be that those memories fuse with reality, and create a darker image in my sleep. I'm safe nowhere. Then she calls my phone, and I realize, I'm awake, and sometimes I wish that it was the other way around.

Softly

Two, maybe three in the morning, and my mother is woken up. Her mother's voice was calm, and she smelled like lilac, but her eyes were full of fear masked with smeared mascara. She's always tried to be one thing to herself, and another to the world. She didn't need to say it, I think they both knew. She smiled a soft smile and kissed my mother's forehead gently, "I love you Krystol." If one word could be used to describe my grandmother, it would be gentle, or perfect. At least on the outside that is.

I imagine that my mother turned on her bedside lamp, as my grandmother closed the door softly, not to wake my aunt and uncle. I'm sure she could hear the car start, and her mother's search beginning. Another night, same routine. I imagine her lying awake, her favorite boy band posters glowing from the lamp, while clenching her stuffed animal kept under the white ruffled pillow. I think about how my grandmother's absence made her come up with lies to tell her siblings as to why both of their parents weren't home, if one of them were to wake up, like a mama bear protecting

8

her young. The job of the oldest she would tell me in defense of

her parents.

Another sleepless night, and the soft pitter patter of rain on

her window. Nana on her infamous hunt, but instead of treasure,

just an overly drunk husband in a lonely bar lying in his own vomit.

V for Villain

They smelled of cheap perfume and cigarettes as they drove down a lightly lit one lane road leading to the only movie theatre in town. The radio blasted "You Give Love a Bad Name" or some other overly played song of the 80's and it was just another Friday night date between my mother and her boyfriend Blaine.

Another Friday where Nana sat at home waiting for Pawpaw, my grandfather to return, and another Friday where he drank her away with his mistress slut of the week. He was predictable. Same place every Friday, and the town knew, but Nana pretended they didn't in order to cling to whatever family dignity they had left.

"Hey, isn't that the place your dad always goes to?" Blaine asked in a joking manner, but mom ignored him as they drove that small town.

"Actually, fuck it, turn around."

"Krystol…"

"Blaine, turn the car around, I just want to see if their cars are there." Blaine turned up the music to tune her out, slid a gentle hand to her knee, a soft wink, and whispered,

Blaine turned up the music to tune her out, slid a gentle hand to her knee, a soft wink, and whispered with his raspy voice, "Look, let's just get on with our date, what would you even-"

Turning down the radio she said, "If you don't turn this car around, I'll get out and walk at the next light." I like to think she started unbuckling her seatbelt, ashing her cigarette, and unlocking the door to manipulate him just enough to get her way.

Her hands got clammy, the kind that you'd be embarrassed to let anyone hold because how could one human ever produce that much sweat. Her heart raced, and she become fixated, not on if he was there or not, but rather if her hero still wore a cape. One that seemed at the time to have been put at the back of a closet or lost at the cleaners, but the short turn-around revealed the truth.

Both their cars, a silver mercedes, and a white one to match sat beside each other, and she double check the license plates. Front and center to the door, he had no shame.

Storming out of the car, she said it was all a blur. A black hole in time between leaving the car and seeing his drunk Wild Turkey veined body leaned over the bar talking to her. He turned and saw her. His eyes grew so large that they could have exploded to see his five foot 16 year old, brown haired, blue eyed, pale, freckled faced daughter standing in that bar, his bar. Blaine darted to the bathroom knowing that that would be a scene, knowing that she had a revenge driven mind, and a heart full of sorrow .

He grabbed her shoulder and threw her into a red seated booth as hard as he could. Scared that the only friends he had in those four walls would strip him of his "secret" life he thought he lived.

"You will go home," he hissed.

"No," she began, "you are going to get your ass in your car and I am going to follow you all the way home."

I like to think he knew he couldn't argue, that she was a ticking time bomb with a lit fuse surrounded in a smoked filled room. He got up, stumbling a little, heading towards the door, but the mistress was still sitting there, and she saw it as her chance.

Mom walked up, head a little higher, fist clinched a little harder. If she could have been any animated character, she would have been the one with steam coming out of their ears.

"Now, Krystol, it isn't going to help to get angry," she spoke in a hushed southern drawl.

Mom's arm pulled back, knuckles of white, and he stepped in front of her. "We're leaving," my grandfather said, but she shook him off, lunged forward, the shot glasses rumbling, and stared eye to eye with her villain.

"We're leaving," she repeated.

Love at First Sight

I wish I could tell you that my parents met by love at first sight, a friendly football game on a Friday night under high school lights, or even bumped into each other through mutual friends but that isn't the case. I wish I could tell you the story that my parents tell everyone, including me. Where my mom was best friends with his younger brother's girlfriend, and his brother. That they met when they both were asked to be in the wedding years later, and that they dated ever since, but that isn't the truth. The truth is years before, when my mother hung out with my future uncle and aunt, they called upon my dad for their weed and alcohol. "Your uncle was the only one with an older brother who could buy it for us," she chuckled with drugged out eyes, and brown teeth.

Reflections on Mom

I talk about my mom like she is dead, but she is very much alive. My mom used to be beautiful, everyone tells me I look just like her, but all I see now is wash away features and drug stained teeth. I found that beauty in a picture once, in one of my random baby books, and I stole it, framed it, and gave it to her, so her beauty and happiness would forever exist in something. My mom would always drink two cups of coffee in the morning in her red robe, and would yank on my feet until I would wake up. My mom used to vacuum the room when I slept, because she said I could sleep through anything. "Do not pass go and do not collect 200 dollars," would be her go to saying when I was approaching "the line," whatever that line might be. My mom would crawl into my bed at night when her husband would snore so loudly that she would lie awake for hours, and I will always remember the smell of her hair on my pillow. My mom watched all of my latest obsessions in tv shows and movies, and actually had a list of her favorites. Well, to be fair, she made lists of everything, and I do it too, and dad frowned upon it because it reminded him of her. One day, I found a book of her lists, including a journal entry of how her husband of the time beat her, I don't know if I believe it or not, it is sad to say. But my mom lied about my dad abusing her during their divorce, so she could get custody, and more child support. I don't think he will ever forgive her, or all the family members who went on stand and participated in the lie. She to this day will admit to it. And on days when her husband and her screamed, she would come sit in my bedroom, and twirl her wedding ring around on her finger. Your dad still loves me, she would tell me, he still wants me, and then she would fall asleep. She used to sleep a lot, and when she didn't it was my favorite time. In those times, she would get waves of wanting to be a mother, and would try to cook. My mother could burn water. She used to try and make this pineapple with mayonnaise and cheese, and one time when she did we all threw it out the window in the dining room when she wasn't looking. But I remember so much more. The way she laughed, the way she cried, even the way she applied her chapstick. Three swipes down, two up, and one all around. And through it all she still would tell me, "The day you were born was

the happiest day of my life," and I believe her.

Black and White

I came at 10:51 am on November 13th, and no matter how much they argue Mom swears it was a Thursday. She reminds me every year that it was exactly 34 hours of back labor, and that it never fails that her back hurts every year on my birthday "like clockwork." Dad tells me that I was so small he could lay me on his arm, head in palm, my feet barely reaching his elbow, 6 lbs exactly according to mom. I've heard the stories of how her ankles were so swollen that dad tried his hardest to put shoes on her feet, then had to leave them because the baby was coming, she was sure of it, but home they returned. Two days later, I came. Exactly on your due date, a rare thing, she reminds me. A nursery black and white, filled with love, and Dr. Seuss illustrations.

But the only black and white I remember is the one that comes to me like a dream. Staring up into our skylights, age 2, as dad moves out, never to enter again. And there it goes, like a fuzzy snapshot from a movie, playing over and over.

Willow

She was the kind of mom who kept a scrapbook of every year of my life. A pink one with diaper pins for the first year. A teddy bear for age 2, angels for age 4, a flower for age 5, a simple color here and there for a few years, and as I get older, they dwindle, getting darker with the ages.

We were the best of friends. We even had a pillow to document it. A little pink one that sat on my bed with a picture of our trip to Miami, laughing with each other, sunglasses and bathing suits. Princess it was captioned in pink cursive writing and bedazzled little flowers. Sometimes, when I was scared, or we fought, I thought about how happy we were on the boat, sun and skin intermingled, the only worry was who would be the first to throw up from getting sea sick.

We had willow tree statues of a mother and her daughter that sat on the top of our entertainment center, that wiggled a little and I was always scared would fall off when I opened up the doors to watch Fairly Oddparents in the morning with a bowl of frosted mini wheats prepared for my arrival. On commercials she would join me so we could switch back to the news, a compromise that went on every week day.

On the weekends, I sat in my yellow colored playroom, with bookshelves built to the ceiling. Drake and Josh episodes on the TV, stuffed animals in all crevices of the room. When nighttime hit, and the distinct smell of fettuccine came from the kitchen, I would run in on the black and white colored tile and grab the bacon bits from the fridge. With a little sprinkle, I would add the extra touch as if that meant the fettucini alfredo was complete, and I helped make dinner.

Our little life was simple. We took apples to the horses in the area where our neighbors yard lined up with ours, and we adopted the neighborhood cat, named him Tiger. My pink Barbie bicycle ruled the neighborhood, and I hung out until dark with my friends, knowing that a simple holler from the door meant dinner was ready and it was time to say goodnight.

When it rained and summer nights of fireflies, sidewalk chalk, and sunburnt skin were tampered with, we played intense games of war. She was the only one with ample amounts of patience to play a game such as this, and carry it through all the way, instead of saying "we'll continue it later" like most monopoly games go for so many. And when the storms persisted, and turned into nights where the windows quivered in the anger of thunder, I would crawl in her bed and read books with the crack of bathroom light. "It's just people in the sky bowling, sweetie. Strike!" she would say as her overly chapsticked lips, and brown messy hair greeted my forehead as she pulled me in.

On holidays, like Valentine's we would make a treat of it. We would go to the grocery store, allowing me to get my very own "little helper" cart where I could pick out the best valentine's day cards, for competition with all the other girls in my class. The scented ones were my favorite, and they had to have the red heart stickers that I could seal them with. We would continue through the aisles, until we came across the sugar cookies that had the designs on them of hearts, the ones that were specific for every holiday, and always seemed to taste better because of it. After our tiring trip, we would go back home, place the cookies in the oven, and sit at the clear kitchen table, filling out the cards, returning days later to vote on who had the best ones this year.

On Christmas, I would wake up and choose to go out the door that lead to the front foyer instead of the typical one through my connecting bathroom. I would swing it open, fuzzy socks on my feet, and slide across the wood floors, for ultimate slickness. Yelling from the kitchen that "You are going to bust your head open," was protocol for such an event, but it was okay because it was Christmas, and it was our tradition.

Nothing could break us up, but she wasn't my hero. She was my confidant, and best friend. She didn't wear a cape, and fight off villains in my drawings, or solve all my problems, but she was my mom. She took me to blockbuster, and we picked out movies, made a pallet fort on the floor of pillows and blankets, and ate whatever food we wanted when it was just "a bad day." We ordered pizza of disgusting flavors just to give them a try, and we jammed out to Ashley Tisdale cds in parking lots late at night.

With the introduction of a baby bump and a new bed keeper, fettuccine nights became sporadic, playrooms were moved to garage corners, scrapbooks became black, and the

thunder grew louder.

First Memory

We run for a van. I keep bouncing up and down on my father's shoulders as we run over pebbles, mulch, and grass lumps that decorate the bright playground of the elementary school. The van peers out a little bit from the trees it hides behind. A flash or two of the lights signify that it is there and ready for the move.

"You son of a bitch!" she screams behind us, running in her white and black colored flip flops and long dress. She matches a monster I once identified as my mother, but now seems to be morphing into a stranger who trails behind.

Dad starts picking up speed as her footsteps increase, getting louder and louder, the only noise now, followed by heavy breathing. I turn my head, eyes widening, face becoming aware, confused, then scared. Her eyes widening also, but this time as if she is a hawk who spots her prey. Her face getting red, her voice getting breathy. My baby hair blows in my face, but I can see that she is gaining on us, and she has a plan. I can see it in her eyes.

With a heavy push, like a linebacker ready to take out an opponent on a field, she hurls herself at us, I come tumbling down, a hard fall that dad tries to control, but without any luck we land abruptly on the hard ground. His ankle twists from a single rock, my body landing feet from his, his Nokia grey phone slides out of his pocket.

"Daddy!" I scream, but he does not respond, and somehow in the wake of his absence, of his consciousness, I feel as if the phone is acting as a bridge between us. Though he can't talk, or cry, or assure me everything is okay, he is with me.

I open my eyes again, but my vision keeps coming in and out, as I drift in and out of consciousness. The definition of his body, blurry then clear, there then completely disappears behind the blackness that consumes my sight, a slight ringing in my ears. Dad continues lying there on the ground, his head pounded into the red clay that makes up North Carolina's soil. I can hear the sound of honking from the van that still sits there waiting, but no one else is around, no birds, no kids, no people. Mom leans down to pick me up, and all I can see is there is no regret nor sympathy in her eyes. I kept looking over at the phone that represents the connection between us, as if we are tied to it and my strings are breaking one by one with each step that we take. Me in her arms, I still wonder what is going on.

A few years later, I was given the Nokia phone as a "present." I could play with it and pretend to call anyone I wanted, Dad told me as he tried to sell me on the gift. I still have that grey Nokia, with its permanent blue crack in the screen, still too scared to get rid of it, feeling guilty I guess as for never playing with it.

Peppermint Patties

The car is silent, the world is silent, just for a second, and there is something special about it. The sun peers through the child safety crack of my window, and it warms me until my goosebumps go away. The wind, like an enemy, blows my hair in several directions, and I can't see but it is okay, because I feel like a diamond when the sun kisses my skin, my freckles like sparkles.

We drive the same roads we do every Tuesday, but something is different about this day. I attend the same ballet class, carry the same navy blue dance bag that contains my very tiny ballet shoes that the bow never seems to stay tied on, and ends up in just a mess of a knot. I wear the same pink tutu, and the same pair of tights that I fight her on every day, because I hate the way they make my skin itch.

The only noise comes from the radio, Avril Lavigne singing in her Canadian accent, and I think of my brother, and how my dad picks on him for denying the fact that she is one of his favorite artists. I think of Chandler, my best friend, and how we dance in my living room to this song, and how mom lets me wear whatever clothes I want when we do that.

We make a turn, and I slide a little, because I am too tiny for this blue clothed seat I sit in, and the buckle just doesn't seem to fit correctly. We pull into Carter Brothers, the place we stop for the best hush puppies and sometimes on dance days mom lets me get french fries too because "I earned them after burning so many calories," whatever that means. As we wait in line, we sing Complicated at the top of our lungs, mimicking her accent, and today is just another Tuesday.

When we get in line, at a certain point, I know it's my cue. I unbuckle, crawl to the front to see if Tabitha is working drive thru, my babysitter. If she is, that means she will sneak me a York peppermint patty and one for mom, and if she isn't, we try again next week.

We get our food, no patties today, but there are french fries. Avril no longer plays on the radio, but I see mom in the rear view mirror, and she smiles a soft smile at me.

"Buckle up Hay. We'll try again next Tuesday," she says as she winks at me, pulling out of the shade, and the sun kisses me again.

Blue

Blue rooms. Blue eyes. Blue skies.

I walk into her bedroom to gather my books from the night before of sleepless slumber. A Dr. Seuss book at the end of the bed, and another book somewhere, but where? I lift up all the covers, searching frantically. I look at the trundle at the end of the bed, and evaluate how it is always locked, like a treasure box, but I don't know if I will ever know what it contains. These newly painted walls are now blue, and it makes the room dark, making my search more difficult.

I throw my tiny body under the bed, inching closer in like an explorer, or one of those people that works under cars, looking, but no find. I look everywhere and nowhere, but it doesn't exist. I call out for help, I just got this book, brand new, all mine, not his. Not the baby's.

She isn't here, I can't find her, and I can't find it. In the midst of my search for no specific reason at all, I go to her bathroom of baby blue, the window open, a bluebird sitting perched on the top of the work shed in the back yard, chirping for the new skies. It tickles my nose and I smell it.

The distinct smell of cigarettes, the distinct smell of change. The baby cries. "Mom!" I call out, as if I didn't know that she was just below the window, her smoke blowing in the blue bathroom. "Umm, yes, Hailey? Yeah, uh I'll be right in," I hear her shuffle, stomping it out, smothering her lies in the dirt. Blue like my great grandfather's skin when he died of lung cancer, and blue like my grandfather's lighter fluid flicks on his cigarette.

Blue. The overcast skies disappear, the grey toned walls of her bedroom change, and six months later his eyes still match mine. The missing book sitting perfectly on the bathroom sink, Stellaluna, and its blue cover.

Katie

Everything is black, and the roads are slippery. People crash into trees, and the sky is lit up by angry screams and bolts of lightning. The only light in the car coming from the tip of her burning cigarette, and the three second snapshots when the sky goes from black to purple and grey. As the thunder grows, her barks get louder, as if on cue.

"Shut the fuck up!" she screams at my dog sitting in the back of the car, trapped in her black crate.

Mom's face lights up in the rear view mirror, and I am scared to look at the monster that has taken over her.

We drive what feels like a short distance, everything looking the same: nothing. But the clock now reads 8:34, and time goes by faster than I thought. Mud splashing up on the white car, we swerve off the road.

She slams the stick into park, and hops out, leaving the door wide open, rain spilling inside, three seconds of light coming here and there, and I am alone.

"Mom! Mom!" my panicked scream shaking the car, tears that taste like salt when they reach my little pink lips, a thin layer of clear lip gloss from last years stocking. The dog keeps pushing against the sides of her crate trying to escape. Pieces of her hair flying around in the air and she is just as scared as me. Something is comforting about that. She sticks her cold black nose through a square in the crate, and touching it lets me know that someone else is there, just in case when she left the car this time, she actually won't be coming back.

We sit here for what feels like hours, but this time, time runs slowly, and the clock reads 8:37. The dog whimpers, and I cry. A team she and I, ever since the first day I got her.

I remember it like it was yesterday. I had just returned from my dad's house, and it was in the stages of when my parents were in constant competition with each other for who could be the cooler parent. Mom always seemed to win because she truly was the only one competing. She told me to go sit on my green swingset. Plastic, it had a single swing, a rocker thing, and a slide, and at the time it was more than enough. She told me she would be right back and went around our one story white paneled home. I sat there where the horses gathered in the neighbor's yard, where yellow tulips bloomed, where I crashed my bike, and where life seemed to begin and end for flowers, a dog, and a little girl.

Mom came around the corner with her, on a blue leash, but really she was walking mom more than anything. She tugged, and red clay and grass flung up under her little paws. Finally, she broke free, running straight for me, licking my knees, and running circles around the playset.

"Katie!" I screamed out as she ran towards me, naming her, bonding instantly.

My heart jumped as the back of the car swung open, as I left my dreamlike memory and returned to the present. There she stood. Mom. Hair wet, hanging like little strands of spaghetti. Clothes almost a little too see through, and flopping around, makeup running down her cheeks.

"Get out! Get out of the damn car" she yelled at Katie as she tussled at the cage lock.

"Mom!"

The bolts of lightning lit up her face as she grabbed Katie by her blue collar, throwing her on the side of the road, her tan chow fur and slick tail changing colors as the mud splashed all over her body.

"What are you doing? Mom! Mom!" I scream as she throws herself back into the front seat.

Reaching over in the glove compartment, pulling out a cigarette, lighting it with a single flick of a blue lighter, and switching the stick to drive.

"If you don't stop crying, you'll never get another dog."

8: 51. We told everyone she ran away.

Noah

The kids run across the hot black asphalt, either to after school programs, or to the car rider line, dresses swaying, coats dropping, it is 3 pm exactly, and school is over for the day. I dodge the kids and their books, their moms' nice cars, and their dads who flirt with the married teachers, heading towards the pre school building where Noah is.

I'll pick both of you up in that line, my mother told me everyday, just in case I forgot the previous day was the same routine. That way she could wear ripped pjs covered in cigarette burns when she picked us up, or shorter shorts than the other moms, and didn't have to walk in and check him out. I'll call and let them know you have my permission to check him out she tells me.

So I walk. Passing playground sets, and teachers, and even the high school building. Vikings the side of the building says, and everything is a deep blue and awful yellow. I walk down the hallway, passing little kids who scream, their book bags bigger than their little bodies.

"Hi, I'm here to...to...Noah," I stutter and rub my elbow, looking at my feet, "I'm here to get Noah, I mean."

"Ah, yes, can you come with me, please?" the middle aged, white, married schoolteacher says as she places a pencil behind her ear.

I follow her around the corner, down the hallway of finger paintings, and stale yellow cement walls, to the bathroom. "He had an accident today, and I need you to clean it up."

"My mom is coming to get us right now, I'll just tell her about it," I say as I grab his small wrist, that matches mine in freckles and color, leading him out of the bathroom.

"No," she begins, "we can't release him until it is clean. Here," she hands me wipes and a diaper.

"I've never changed him before," I start to cry, "can you please help me?"

"Sorry I am not allowed to touch him, it is a requirement for children to be potty trained before they are enrolled," she says as she closes the door, locking it from the outside, "so no one will come in, I'll be on the other side."

The clock passes, 3:15…3:20 and the cracks in the blue and yellow tile remain as I sit against the door still crying for help. 3:21 and I bring Noah into a small, crowded stall that smells of pee from missed targets, and clumps of hair that hide in corners. No one can get in, no one can get out. But I like the privacy that the stall door gives, even if I can see over the top of it. 3:23 and I finally give in.

Start changing him, I think to myself. My hands shake as I gently pull down his grey elastic pants, revealing a Mickey and friends diaper, and it's number 2 he whispers to me. As I take off the diaper, brown smudges going all the way up to his stomach, hours of wiggling around in filth, I lean over the toilet in fear I might puke. Crying, and shaking, I stand there, staring at his little body. This is disgusting I scream to myself as I grab a wipe and his penis changes from a dark brown, to a soft white. I yell at him, "I'm never doing this again! Do you hear me?" But his big blue eyes stare back at me, like little holes of emptiness.

I repeat, "Never again," and I throw away the mess, and wash my hands, scrubbing with soap until my hands turn red, crying and singing to myself my ABC's in the mirror. 3:28 and I

bang on the door with red eyes and peppermint hands. The lock

unlatches. "All done?" she smiles, and I step around her, feeling

like the biggest person in this small hallway.

We leave finally, and mom waits in her car for us. I tell her

what happens and she doesn't even say thank you, or I am sorry.

"Maybe you should potty train him too, he listens to you better than

me anyway." And I buckle the seat belt, and we leave. 3:34 and all

the kids are gone.

Hidden Treasure

It was a Christmas like no other, Santa wasn't coming this year they said. "Don't expect a lot under the tree," I heard mom say countless times, and I told her it was fine, but deep down I wondered why it was this way. We decorated the tree with the same ornaments, and though I hated decorating I did it anyway because we were spending time together. Tree sap smelling, cookies baking, Christmas movies playing-kind-of-time, and those were the most memorable and rare in my eyes. Like routine, I went and put on my pjs when we returned from my grandparents house, where we celebrated with them but not a second too late because we would turn on the news and wait to see when the weathermen said Santa was getting close. I came down in my fleece lined ones, new for the occasion, tradition.

Sit down, she would say to my siblings and I, because each year on Christmas Eve we would get to open up one present of our pickings. 3 for each of us this year, and one I knew would be an ornament for the tree, it always is, and will never fail to be. We gather around on our living room rug, and we sit all together, the baby still too young to understand. I look at the boxes, and bows, and decorations and try to decide which one is the ornament, because no one wants to open that, or socks, what fun is that?

This year, she begins, you and J don't get to pick them out, I want you to open these together, and she handed us small boxes. When she looked under the tree again to make sure it was the right one, I shook it a little to try and figure out what was in it. I wasn't the kid who snooped around the house, I liked surprises, typically.

On the count of three, she began, and the excitement built up. It was a race, and I had to be in first. We started ripping through the wrapping and tissue paper, and when we opened it up, there was a slip of paper. Blank stares, and confused eyes glanced at her, fearful to ask what we just received. I looked at J, three years older than me, but even an 11 year old had no idea what our hands rested on. She snatched them up, trying to sell us, and herself on what we received. "It's a receipt honey, you and J now have your very own savings funds." "What's a saving fund?"

"You'll appreciate it when you're older," and she tucked it back

away under the tree.

It must be an imaginary bank she set us up with, or the

money is buried deep deep down in bags of snow.

I Owe You

I owe you
A penny, a dollar,
A lifetime of debt
My love, my attention,
I owe you

I owe you
A Ten,
Then twenty,
Quickly to thirty
Ending in forty,
Jumping to 80
I owe you

I owe you
Your childhood,
Your innocence,
Your pain,
Your love
I owe you

I owe you
Hidden in a drawer
Hidden in a closet
Hidden under the bed
I owe you

A slip of paper,
"I owe you", it wrote.

The Rising Sun

I watch her leave. The car lights shine through the windows as she drives away, the shadows wrapping their arms around me.

How long she will be gone this time I don't know. She did this a lot now, leaving without a clue of where she is going or for how long. I grab the blanket to soak up my tears. Tears from screaming "Mommy please don't go, please, I promise I'll do whatever you need." The tears that follow when the door comes to a close, and the tears when the rattling of the car can't be heard anymore.

My brother, Noah, sits in the recliner with his stuffed toy dog, Thomas the Train matching pajamas, and singing along to Dora. His innocent eyes cut across to me. "I'm hungry." As usual, I get up, go into the kitchen, looking for something I could give him, to make a "dinner."

I open the fridge: nothing but juice. I open the freezer: nothing but ice. I open the pantry: nothing but unused trash bags, expired cans of baked beans, and a broom. I open the cabinets:

nothing but pepper. Then I repeat it all as if something might appear.

Running around the kitchen, slamming cabinets, "We will eat soon I promise," I yell to the next room. I open the door leading to the garage seeing if something is accidentally placed there, then I look through my book bag that sits on the bench in the room. Hoping. Hoping I have stuffed away a snack for when I was really hungry. Nothing. What was I to do? He has to eat. I can hear him getting restless in the chair. I can last until morning, when she will return, but he can't. He walks into the kitchen, sitting on the wooden bench staring. His eyes like daggers.

I return to the pantry, grabbing the can, running my hands around the paper looking for the expiration date, just in case I got it wrong. It isn't there. I flip the can over. Expired two years ago. I begin to question how sick we might get if we eat the expired beans, a few months probably isn't *that* expired after all. But in fear that we might get sick, in fear of having to take care of him all night, in fear of hospitals, I decide to call her.

I call, and call, and call again. Each time my fingers press a little harder on the keys, hands shaking a little more, and every time no response. I hang up the phone, returning to the four year old now screaming in a shrilling cry of hunger. I grab him, holding him close, trying to stop him from fighting me off. "Shh...it's okay, I'll figure it out. Shh. Please. Look if you stop crying I'll let you stay up a little later. Just. Shh."

I open the pantry again to the beans. I check the trash. I almost call dad, but after dialing the number, immediately hang up because I know I will get in trouble if she knew he got involved.

"Don't ever call your dad and tell him what goes on over here, he'll take you from me, and you wouldn't want to hurt Mommy, right?" she always asks me. But I have to. No. I can't. She needs my help. Noah needs me. I can't call. She says it will get better. Dad won't believe me, and if I went to live with him she might get sad again and never get out of bed. She might never come back.

I call my brother, my half brother, my father's son, for help.

I remember eating a 16 year old's budgeted Wendy's dinner of a cheeseburger with onions. I hate onions, but right now I've never been so thankful. He chomps away at his kids meal, and I think to myself, "this beats baked beans."

I remember two rounds of the sun rising before she came back.

Goodnight

"Sit here," mom says as she gets out of her black BMW station wagon, parked at the top of our driveway, slamming the door. She slams the door so hard that it shakes the inner rearview mirror, and the cup from McDonald's earlier that day. We were having such a good day, but things were about to change, I could feel it in the slam of the door, and the way she ran down the driveway. Even the way the springtime night air feels as it rushes into the car.

The headlights of the car flash against our garage doors, and at the bottom stands Todd, her husband, my brothers dad, who's been gone all day, not answering the phone when mom called about a thousand times as we ran errands. Once when we started passing out the flyers for his business, once when we went and got a special treat at Mcdonald's for helping, and about every other time Noah said "mailbox" in a neighborhood whose yards were approximately 20 feet from the next.

Noah starts to squirm in the backseat and I can tell that at any second he will want to get out, but we can't. I watch her as she approaches him, red eyed and screaming. I watch him change from the guy who lets me sit on his lap and watch movies, who calls me "his girl" to an equally red eyed monster, screaming, louder and louder.

"Hey, wanna listen to the blue song?" I turn around to face him in the back seat, jittery and wide eyed, trying to mask the screams coming from outside. I turn on the inside lights, and search around for the disk that contains his favorite song. Putting it in the slot, and pressing play he says, "Why is it so loud?"

"A dance party," I say as I begin to dance in an over the top way so he would do the same. His small body wiggles in his car seat, and I make funny faces to distract him and make him laugh.

Her wedding ring glistens in the headlights from the car, his missing. He corners her, against his truck, face so close to hers it looks like he's about to eat her. Finger right between their eyes. I don't know what is being said, but I know it's not good. He slams her harder against the truck, arms waving in the air, and she is trying to escape to us.

"Hey watch this," I say and grab his stuffed animal now making him dance, because I'm losing my audience, and the outside world is one he shouldn't see. We sit there, and the song continues, *I'm blue ba da be...*

The door swings open, "Get inside" she screams at me.

"Mom...Mom..."

"You heard me, grab your brother and get inside."

His lights turn on, and he floors the gas, backing up, mom jumping out of the way. "Now Hailey!"

I jump out, open the door, unbuckle him, tell him to put his face in my shoulder and run, like the wind, like I'm running from something, or someone, but I don't know which.

I place him inside, and close the door, as she runs down the street after his truck. "Todd!" she screams, and I turn out the porch light, locking the door. Goodnight.

When I Thought She was Anorexic

Her grey skin,
Matching the skies,
And the grey in her eyes

She holds a baby
Too big for her small
Small, body

Her bones, fragile,
Blow in the wind,
Whisks of body odor,
Chapstick,
And decay
Join the springtime air

They blossom,
And bloom,
And she,
Like a tree whose roots are dug up
Is no longer grounded

Slipping day by day
To her grave

White powder
So they say,
The white enemy,
Others may

Lost in herself,
Anorexia for those,
 Who don't know,

That a bump in the night
Cures the morning,

And the grim reaper stands weeping,
For another day passes,
And she,
Not his victim

Red Sacs and Gas Stations

I clear my throat.

The water is teal blue and the outside lights softly illuminate the water of the deep end. The smell of chlorine mixes perfectly with the smell of the sticky hot air of a typical summer night. Maroon 5 plays softly in the background, but I tune it out. I want to say it, but the water is calm. It moves in small ripples by the movement of my legs, and the water bugs glide on them like tiny surfers.

My dad stands at the stainless steel grill. "Ah," he begins with a sip of his beer, "it sure is a beautiful night," he says as he looks up at the clear night sky decorated with stars. Now is my chance, but the water is becoming cold, and there are mosquitoes. I let him continue.

"Anything new?" he continues with the swift turn of the tongs to pork chops.

"Umm, nothing really." Lie.

"Come on now Bug, there's bound to be something."

"Not really." Lie again.

We sit in silence, the awkward kind, and I pull my legs out of the water, letting the small droplets of water run down them. I turn and look at him. He stands looking up at the night sky, with hands placed on hips. The sky like a void of nothingness, then there is a star. Now two, and three, as my eyes come to adjust.

Now is my chance. I clear my throat. I feel my heart beat a little faster. I step over the black hose that resembles a slippery snake, and lies where the crack in the cement is. He still stands there, "it's a nice night out."

"Yeah, it is," I start in a rushed manner, "Dad…" I begin as he throws the hood of the grill up, startled by noise and the warmth of the flames that carry the heat of summer and the smell of charred meat. The song switches and I lost my chance. "Smells good," I continue.

I pat his shoulder as I turn to walk back inside. Stepping back over the snake hose, and heading towards the door, my hand nears the door handle, and I begin to give the extra push necessary to pry the door from its jam.

"Bug."

"Yeah?"

"Where are you going?"

"Inside."

"No, stay out here it is nice out."

Our bodies stand uncomfortable and stiff beside each other, staring in the direction of the road that is blacked out by the night sky. The crickets chirp, and the bats dive at the water bugs on the pool water. The smell of sweat fills the air, and I know. I know everything is going to be different now.

She keeps coming back in flashbacks, sudden images like a movie projector of old family films that only seem to play in my head. She'll hate me, I think to myself, they all will. Then as if the other angel sitting on my shoulder says, but you have to. Sometimes it has to be about you.

"Dad..."

"Is there something wrong?" We speak a little too softly at the same time.

I clear my throat.

"Dad, you've got to get me out of there."

We continue staring at the absence of road.

"It's time."

He shifts his stance, looking at me, and without any other questions or remarks, he knows. Something about my eyes, the fear in my voice, or maybe the desperateness. With a deep sigh and shut of the lid of the grill, he clears his throat holding back tears, fear, and his own sense of desperateness.

"I knew this day would come. I'm sorry, babe, I have been waiting so patiently since you were two."

"It's worse than you think, Dad. I don't tell you everything. I tried telling Nana and she wouldn't listen. I cried and begged her." My face gets hotter with every word, and each one gets a little harder to say.

"Well, your grandmother," he says with a pause.

"Dad, I don't want to go back."

"Hey. Look. Stop crying. Here's what we will do. You know those woods at the end of your street?"

I nod.

"You walk through there, and you keep walking, all the way to my house."

"Dad, that's a long walk."

"Then you call. I bought you a phone to call me."

"But she monitors my calls, and she'll follow me."

"Then you leave at night, and you walk to the gas station, and you ask to borrow a phone, and you call me, I'll be there, always."

We continue to look at the black sky and lack of road.

****

Sometimes, I would lie in my bed at night for hours, and stare at that blacked out road, and picture me walking down it with a red sac on a stick.

April 6, 2010

...Can't wait ya'll get to pick me up tomorrow for dinner. I hope if you're having any problems with me being here, I hope you are talking to Nana or Todd about it. Please baby don't hold it in, it's not good at all. I think when I get out we are going to go to the beach...we need some family healing time.

Daymark

The wind blew softly through the trees as if it was soothing nature with a lullaby to awaken the day. The few wisps of baby hair blew across my face, curly and untamed. It was the kind of day that if you stood in the sun you were warm because it kissed your skin and provided a thin layer of protection, but if you crossed over to the shade then the true temperature presented itself.

I stood there in my "Sunday Best," as southerners would call it. This consisted of a pastel dress that almost touched my knees. It was a light peach color, with embroidered flowers that met the base of my chest right where my breast would start. I had shaved my legs, smooth to the touch, my nails and toes painted, and shown off perfectly behind brown leather sandals. The smell of apples and flowers radiating from my skin due to a cheap perfume that I bathed in.

I gripped the teddy bear between my fingers, and in the cusp of my elbow held a dozen red roses. At any second she could walk through that door, and when she did I didn't know how to react. Was I supposed to smile? Was I supposed to cry? The door creaked open, and though it was glass, I still didn't know who was about to disrupt this calm day; I refused to look up, the whole time focusing on my feet and how they looked in my shoes.

"Happy Easter," an old man with a scruffy voice spoke as he cracked a smile, though I didn't know if he really did or not since I wasn't looking up, but everyone smiles on Easter, right? The sanctity of his voice made me realize that it was safe to look up, because it meant she wasn't here yet, and I had a few more minutes to prepare myself for this.

As my eyes met with his, they drifted towards his white beard, containing food tangled within it, his stained shirt, and greased hat. She stood behind him. Two came through that door, but hid behind the voice of one. My heart stopped beating as if time itself stopped entirely. I looked around for an escape, for the backyard seemed so much smaller, as if it was all closing in on me.

The simple chirps of the birds began to increase and sound more like screeches, shrieks, and an overall eerie sensation that seemed to make my entire body tingle from one tip of the spine to the next. My palms became sweaty, my heart rate came back all of a sudden and beat like a giant bass drum. Everything was crashing, all within the span of the ten seconds it took her to walk towards me.

As she went in for a hug, I dropped the teddy bear, and swooped down to save it? I picked it up by its soft fur, and now dirt covered foot, and took a giant step backwards. I pushed the roses to her, refusing to make eye contact. The length of my arm creating the cold distance between us.

"Happy Easter,' I mumbled. My eyes got blurry as tears formed, and I stared at my feet, then hers, and how they looked identical. "The first thing your dad told me when you were born was *well she has your feet*" played on repeat in my head. I held the bear out for her to grab.

She picked up instantly on the clues that I did not want to be touched, and she walked away to the next victim. I released a big sigh, looked down at my hands that were now shaking as if I was standing in Antarctica instead of 70 something degree Greensboro, North Carolina.

Everything went silent. Complete and utter silence, followed shortly by blackness, eyesight completely vanishing. I knew that that was the warning signs of a very disastrous panic attack, so I sat down as gracefully as I could on a black iron seat that set parallel to a matching table, the cold touch calming me.

In the center of that table sat an overly perky bunny holder with decorated eggs holding a stack of pamphlets. "Happy Easter from Daymark Alcoholics and Narcotics. A Happy and Healthy World."

Children's laughter pulled me back in. They ran around with their aunts, uncles, parents, grandparents, cousins, siblings, and relatives. They kissed each other on the lips, and hunted for Easter eggs in the backyard. They climbed up on patched jeans and worn out knees and listened to to stories from stale voices. When it turned one, they all went inside to join the families for lunch, including mine, but I remained staring at the bunny holder.

It was the first time I saw her since she was sent away. It could have been earlier, but I was scared. I still am. I don't know if it is because I am scared that she didn't really change, or that she did and that somehow no longer makes her my mother.

I never came back.

She, however, did five more times to be exact.

Bus Stops

We walk the same trails we do every summer night, or school nights when the winds are still warm, and the trees are still full with leaves. This time he suggests we make a left hand turn on our trail instead of a right, but that scares me, unknown paths I whisper. Hailey, we made the paths, he says laughing, and I follow him. He is leaving soon, in a few weeks to be exact, and when he does home won't feel the same anymore. He is my best friend here, the one who holds all the secrets about what really happens behind the dogwood trees, and red painted door. Where the screams really come from in the night, and the reason why we really created this path. He keeps telling me not to worry, we both have to leave Hidden Valley he reminds me. The street we currently call home, but in these next few weeks I'll live with Dad, and he'll be gone. No more pool days, no more Dr. Peppers and sneaking into houses being built. We keep walking and we see it. The house that contains all the mysteries, the one where all the poisonous snakes breed apparently. In the middle of a field of flowers, wood rotting on the side, no road to connect to it. Free and alone, we sit here in front of the house, and the grass tickles our legs, but it's okay, because the sun is out and we run and scream. But I just want to go back to awkward first meetings at middle school bus stops.

Sunday Morning

Sunday morning and the sun is peering through the French windows in the dining room, and the house smells of strong coffee beans and bacon. Like usual, we are sitting together, Dad and I watch the Sunday morning show, and I pretend to be interested in it only because he wants to share it with me.

We sit on our red couch, the one that if you lean back too much, the bottom seat cushion pushes out, and the back one is engulfed. Again, Dad gets up, cursing it out, and slamming pillows here and there as he tries to fix it. "I paid too damn much for this to happen as much as it does," I say mocking him as he performs his Sunday routine.

Today is different. The birds are still chirping, and the bacon is still cooking, and we are okay, but the sky is different, and the phone rings.

"Okay, see you soon," he speaks in a hushed tone as he pulls the bacon from the oven, and my small black and white dog barks for a scrap, or two.

"Who was that?"

Silence.

"Dad?"

"Your mom, she wants to stop by."

"Mom?"

"Yeah."

"Why?" I say rolling my eyes in a joking manner, but I turn to see his face is pale, matching the white calvin briefs and undershirt he wears. Gone, like a ghost.

"I don't know. She wouldn't tell me," he lies.

Thirty minutes have passed, and she still isn't here. I have no appetite, and I couldn't tell you what I am even watching on this program. Mom and Dad do not get along, not like "oh they bicker here and there", but like Dad just pretends she doesn't exist, so this was completely out of nowhere. She shows up though, like he said, and she looks like she hasn't slept in months. Her hair, thrown up off her shoulders, a raggedy blue sweater, t shirt, and jeans that haven't seen the daylight from her closet in ten years. I open the door, and the chimes ding as the alarm system recognizes she's there.

She sits down, pretending to be interested in my breakfast still sitting here, but now cold like doll house food on the TV tray. Dad gets up, fumbles around in the kitchen, but clearly listening in to what is going on, as if he is leaving the awkwardness, but there are no walls to block us. Everything is open, one giant room, and the tension rises and expands through it all. She continues with small southern talk of, "so what did you get into this weekend?" as she sits a little too stiff on the couch.

"What's going on?" I say abruptly, knowing that this is too weird of a situation for everything to be okay.

"Well, umm sweetie…" she begins, her hand, long and skinny fingers just like mine, drifts over touching my pale, freckled knee cap, "last night there was an incident."

I swallow, imagining another talk of drug abuse, or something along those lines, and I feel my body change to resemble hers in the awkward, stiff position.

"What incident?" I snark.

"Well, you know how Ninny and Pawpaw have the celebration of tables today? They were at the church setting up, and they got a call from Uncle Johnny saying that their house was on fire, and they needed to get home. They don't know what caused it yet, but they are okay, Ninny and Pawpaw are okay," she says as she turns her dark blue eyes into mine, to make sure I understand this vital piece of information.

"How much is gone?"

"Everything, there's nothing left."

"Everything?" I question softly to myself, but before I can get anything else out, I feel my hands starting to shake, and get clammy. My eyes watering, and I can't stop thinking about the beanie baby collection, or my room. My books, and pink makeup pallets, keepsakes from when I was a kid. My clothes and Christmas gifts, even the train that sat on the mantle during Christmas time. I think of the refrigerator and its constant stock of strawberry applesauce, and the pantry white board that I would draw on. I thought of the back office, and of the bathroom where a grey wet rag would lie beside the sink for me to wash my face at night. I think of the porcelain figures I would play with and always get told to not break. I think of the candy jar that sits on the clear table in the "smoke room." I think of the corner table in the front hallway that is decorated for every holiday and I...

"Gone?" I ask again.

I think about Easter in the backyard, and watching basketball games in the living room. I think of their cat Bootsie, and our hate love relationship.

"Gone," she says.

Dad comes over now, sitting on the other side of me, surrounded, I feel like I can't breathe. My throat is dry, but my eyes are never ending waterfalls. Whatever was left of my parents, is gone. Their wedding albums, my mother's wedding dress, everything. Vanished with the lit of a flame.

"Why are you crying? Didn't you hear your mom? Your grandparents are okay, the house is just gone," Dad speaks now.

"But...that was my house too!" I scream as I stand up, grab the remote, switch it to the news, the story immediately coming on about the "local family fire."

"Get up!" I scream, "I have to fix the couch!"

And just like that, Sunday's become my least favorite day.

Jones

"Would you like something to drink?" my grandmother asks

me as I sit at a cold, white tiled bar on a wobbly stool and look

down at the cracks, the dirt between them, admiring the simplicity

of how they all just seem to fit together. This question immediately

snaps me back to reality.

"Wait, what?" I ask in confusion, tucking my excess hair

behind an ear, looking in the direction of the noise.

"Would you like something to drink?" she repeats herself,

and walks over to the wooden cupboards opening them with her

long orange painted fingernails and wrinkled skin. She searches

around until she finds the one that contains glasses. Hand painted

fish adorning the cups, typical for a beach rental. A house I was

never intended to enter.

At this moment, my Dad turns the corner, opens up the

small excuse for a pantry that squeaks a little when it opens and

requires a special type of tug to make it open. He reaches to the

bottom, grabs a Jones drink and places it on the tile as the glass bottle dings. He cracks a smile, winks his right eye, and says, "Who loves you?"

I sit here, feeling confused, and sorry for myself. The giant elephant sits right in the middle of the room, pink, polka dotted and all, but we continue to look around it. Not because we want to pretend it isn't here, but rather because it isn't the right time to address it.

As my grandmother stands here in the kitchen preparing dinner, she observes me. Crying, though silently to myself, I stare at the drink but won't open it. Maybe it is because I don't think I have any strength, maybe it is because somehow if I open it I will actually have to stop thinking about it. The reason I am here, the reason my father kidnapped me from school, and drove me 6 hours away from it all.

She walks to that same squeaky pantry, and pulls out the biggest box of brownie mix I have ever seen. She places it right in front of me.

"Extra chocolatey," she says with a half smirk, the kind out of pure desperation to bring a smile to someone's face.

"She got arrested," I whisper to myself but in a loud enough tone that she knew I was talking to her. All the while I continue to trace my finger along the dirt filled cracks of the tile, the jones bottle still unopened.

She freezes and looks me in the eyes. I quickly look back down, afraid to show my swollen, bloodshot eyes, and shaky lips.

"She got caught in a drug deal, at our house. The cops were called, Noah was there. He watched the drug deal…" I spoke as I begin to choke up. I clear my throat, close my eyes and breathe deeply.

"He's in temporary custody with social services until someone can be granted guardianship. Noah. Noah was there. He's only 6. He watched." I continue, followed by straight tears, the ugly ones.

She gasps in pure fear, sadness, and shock. "Babe, I don't know what to say. I am so sorry," she continues softly, fighting back her own tears. Her 13 year old granddaughter sitting here, as she watches me crumble and break just like glass upon these tiles.

Sweaty palms, I wipe my tears away. I go to change topics, I feel obligated to tell them how I got here, how I crashed their weekend at the beach.

"I got called out for an early dismissal and I was really confused why mom was picking me up early, because it's her weekend," I start, "then I walked to the front office and saw dad sitting there and I was even more confused. He wouldn't tell me why he was there until I got in the car. I kept asking why he was there, but all he told me was that we would talk about it when we got there. He said that whatever it was it was bad, and Bev had already packed me a bag and we had to leave as soon as we packed the car. That I couldn't tell anyone where I was going, and that we would call Mom once we were far enough away and tell her what happened," I finish quietly, mainly to myself now, staring all the while at the bottle that sits in front of me.

I swiftly grab it by its neck, twist the top off, and read the message on the inside of the lid. *You are surrounded by love.* The cursive black print written on the metal cap, and I look up to see all around me the kitchen now consisting of my Dad, Bev, Gran, and

Pappy. I look at them with teary eyes, and take the first sip of

grape flavored fizz. "Who loves you?" Dad repeats.

"You do."

New Beginnings

It's April. Vulnerable tulips lean towards the sun, opening up and welcoming the day. Dogwoods shade the fresh thin layer of dew covered grass, and butterflies float by whispering of the tiny scream of spring. But I hate this day. It isn't beautiful, the flowers, trees, and butterflies are all lying.

I walk out of my room, peach colored sundress on that will probably be deemed not appropriate by either its straps, or length, or a tiny pick in it that only a certain type of people could identify. I tiptoe to not wake anyone up, but as I turn the corner, entering the living room, and the floor creaks, I smell bacon. Fresh, applewood bacon, maybe some eggs, maybe some gravy, very Sunday morning, very dad.

"What are you doing up so early?" dad asks as he turns the bacon that sizzles on the stove, alarmed by the creak in the floor.

"I told you this dad, celebration of tables."

"Good luck," he speaks in a sarcastic chuckle.

I roll my eyes, "Ya you have that right," a small smirk on my face.

"Mom?"

"Unfortunately."

"Good luck."

I nod.

"Who's getting you?"

"Ninny," I say as I grab the rest of my belongings that sat on the chimney stoop a little too long, heading towards the door.

"Hey Bug…" he starts.

"Ya?"

"You look beautiful."

I smile. Maybe the butterflies aren't lying after all.

****

There is something unique about a church, about a southern baptist church that is, especially on a day like today. All the regular church attending cars pull into the black asphalt parking lot and are all complaining, and talking shit about each other. They all don't want to be here. They aren't here because they want to be "closer to God," or "hear a wonderful sermon," or in this instance "have a day for the women without any men, to celebrate each other and our faith." That's what they tell us, sure, but it couldn't be further from the truth. Every woman is here so Mrs. Frankie and Mrs. Donna and all the other members who run the church know they are.

It is as if, by entering the parking lot, each car opens up the glove compartment and pulls out a mask that they place on their face, accompanied with some baked goods, their pen stricken Bible, and a little southern hospitality. And I, adapt to this environment, not for me, but for my grandmother.

Breathe. Grab things. Go.

"Hello, Ms. Hailey," Mrs. Donna says as we step out of our cars, and just "happen to realize" we have been parked beside each other all this time.

"Hi, nice to see you."

"Oh look at that cute *little* dress, where is your grandmother, do you know?"

"No ma'am, she is quite a social butterfly, I am sure she has already sprinted off to go talk to someone she noticed."

"Ah, I see, well I think I saw your mother over there looking for you sweetie."

"Oh, okay, thanks."

****

We walk into the vibrant room, each table decorated with a theme by a key lady member of the church. Their guests file in, signing into the same book that they have used for twenty years, and look for their table, fake smiles, and laughs here and there on the way to place down their belongings of braided purses, light pink lipstick, and shaws. Butterflies and pastels decorate a table here, symbolizing the feeling of freedom and rebirth after salvation. Ships and anchors decorate another, hinting at the anchoring of your soul to jesus. Nature decorates another, for creation, but I like the most gaudy of them all, I mean at least it is as ridiculous as this entire event.

I however, rearrange the name places on our table so mom doesn't sit beside me, or remotely near. I then proceed to go say hello to all the members of the church who think my dad has made me an atheist. I breeze by my other grandmother who arranges another table, and it is like a yearly competition that neither grandmother discusses, though whichever table I don't sit at means I have somehow royally pissed them off for the year. I can't wait for my aunt to get here, because she is as much of a black sheep in this religion as I am, and at least if we burn, we burn together.

The guests are instructed to return to their tables, getting ready for prayer so we can start eating the same meal we do every year. Chicken salad, arguably the best out of all the options, two types of casserole, cranberry dip, and bread, with sorbet and chocolate crackers for dessert. I sit in the lightly padded seat, adjusting my napkin, smelling the food that is about to be served to us by the volunteering men, who we should be "thankful to" for serving us, as if it is such a crazy thought that women shouldn't always be the ones in the kitchen, serving.

I smell her. Cheap perfume, cigarettes, and bad breath before I see or hear her. "For some reason Ninny didn't put us beside each other, so I rearranged them so I can sit beside my baby," she whispers to me. I nod. Everyone else sits down, and the room goes from a loud roar to a quiet cricket, getting ready to hear the leading prayer, and as we bow our heads, and all the guests sit down, friends and family, she makes a scene. She speaks a little too loudly about the rearranging, and I am too scared to take the brunt, but it is loud and obvious, so I do.

The meal continues, and I am questioned. It always starts with "Well, we haven't seen you in a while," with a soft smile and a glare that could cut you from across the table. Then it traditionally continues with "How is school? You are so smart. Any new boys?" and always ends with, "how is your Dad?" which is a question they don't really care to hear the answer to. Any act of not speaking to Mom is a direct attack, and her anger increases. It becomes a scene of pouting, interrupting, and snide comments. It cumulates to be bigger than it is, and it constitutes yelling, softly, and shushing by my embarrassment. She doesn't care and sometimes I think it must be lonely being the only one in her world.

****

I get told as we clean up, and begin to head over to the church that I must sit beside her, and give her attention because she is my mother. That I must return to Ninny's after and spend the day with the family, but I explain I was here for everyone else not me, and that I have to go home. I get told how awful I am, how I am selfish, and all I care about is dad. Maybe she is right, but sometimes I have to do what is best for me. I remind myself of this as I close my eyes and take deep breaths, trying to avoid panicking. It turns into a loud whisper, then a yell, now everyone is staring. She is angry and I don't think she is even capable of addressing the real issue. But I don't have to be here, so I call dad to come get me. 15 minutes he says for his 30 minute travel.

****

I sit on a rock, the warm breeze, sticky from the humidity, blowing up the skirt of my dress, and I wait. I hear the congregation starting in the main part of the church, but I sit on the side of the road, birds as my symphony. The only thing she is really mad about is that I never want to be around her anymore, and she knows this, but she hopes it will be different. She never thinks about the world she created with the help of her little white enemy, that now rests as the gatekeeper to a world I no longer want to enter. I sit here with the tulips, and admire their vulnerability, how they open in the sunlight, only to find out that it too will leave, and they will close back up when the sky turns grey and cold.

One Step Forward

He delivers the news swiftly, floating off his tongue, and he is tall and I am very very small. He tells me she's back in rehab, involved in drugs again, and I crumble. Something about back to cocaine, something about drinking with it, and I mutter she's better now. Something about her losing her job, having black out states and screaming at coworkers. He unpacks the groceries, and my hands quiver, and I see spots. He unloads the ham, the potatoes for next Tuesday, and a frozen pizza. He unloads red apples, but redder than my hair, and a pineapple. Like the kind she use to make back in the day. Something about how they won't put her in a mental institution even though her parents have tried. Don't repeat that, he says, asparagus, beans, and hominy. Dori barks at a moth, and I ask how long. How long what, he says. How long has this been going on? I continue. My knees buckle, and I fall to the floor.

"Jesus Hailey, are you still really surprised about this? Your mom is never going to get better, one step forward and five steps backwards. Get up. We have dinner to make."

July 7, 2011

...one thing you have to understand is I know I made yet another
mistake. But the extent of it was told to you wrong. It did happen a
couple of times but I was not "back on drugs" like was told to you.
But I did make a handful of mistakes. It was not constant nor even
weekly just a few times a month for the past few months.

The Look

I was asked in middle school to write about the worst conversation you've ever had with someone. It had no guidelines as to what the conversation had to be about, or if it was a grammatical thing, or a basis of a story you once held that was awkward, or boring, or what have you. For most kids my age, it was when they said something incorrectly and everyone laughed at them, or when they didn't make a good grade and their parents got mad, if they got told they wouldn't make a sports team, and so on. We shared these stories in class, and I don't remember the point of this exercise, but I won't ever forget the day, because it was the first time I had ever received *that* look. We went down the aisles, in a overly bright lit room, with white ceramic tiled floors, and cinder block cream colored walls. Typical middle school room, filled with typical middle schoolers. The stories all began to sound the same, and honestly I think the teacher included, began to tune out herself. And then it got to me.

"Okay, Hailey, your turn."

Without hesitation I responded, "The day I confronted my mother about her cocaine addiction." Everyone got silent. So I explained that day as so:

"We had been drifting apart for months. She knew it. I knew it. Actually, the whole family knew it. I knew she had a problem, with drugs I mean, and I knew it was something hard core, but honestly I didn't know what it was. I tried to ask her about it several times, and each time she kept changing the topic, acting as if what I was saying wasn't the truth, and what I was seeing was all made believe.

Then one night, she took me down to my grandparents, which was only about 15 minutes from us, the one whose house burnt down by the way, and it wasn't anything out of the ordinary. We go there all the time for dinner, or to watch movies, just catch up, that kind of thing. So we had a relatively normal dinner, and by normal, well our family seems to have a different definition of that. After we cleaned the table, emptied the scraps into the trashcan, and helped wash the dishes, Mom told me that Pawpaw needed to see me upstairs. So I ran up as fast as I could, thinking that something cool was about to happen, or there was an early birthday surprise or something. Instead I found him sitting at a round wooden table, waiting for me almost, and it threw me off because he never sat there. Ever. In fact, I don't think I have ever seen anything sit there except for papers now that I think of it. The papers that made the space look like it was meant for something, like an office or private study, but it was all a facade. He was a retired old man that sat in a room of brown. Brown walls that were a deeper shade than the original because of the smoke that clung to them, brown furniture with permanent creases and cat hair, and even brown wooden signs that read "Yes, Dear," and "Everyday is Paradise."

"Sit down," Mom says in a stern voice as she approaches behind me.

So I do and I know almost immediately that something is wrong. The whole atmosphere in the room is vastly different than the one downstairs. Even the cat they own runs and hides behind the little couch, and I wish I could hide like the cat.

"Baby, I thought it would be best for Pawpaw to explain to you about my problem," she starts.

My eyes cut across to her in utter disbelief that this is how and when she chooses to do this, and that she is using my grandfather not as someone to explain, but a cop out.

"I thought that maybe you might be confused and that someone in the program can simplify it for you," she continues.

"I don't want to hear it from the program," I say as I cut my eyes across directly to my grandfather, "I want to hear it from you," I shout at my mother while I switch my stare to her. I can feel myself getting really tense, and I start to shake because in a way though I was happy to hear what was going to be said, and to acknowledge that all these years I wasn't crazy, I am also absolutely terrified to admit it was reality.

He tries to ease into the conversation, speaking slowly, and with big words that only people in that program can understand. It isn't coming from the heart, it is coming from the "Big Book." He even starts with the statement, "Well, the Big Book says…" I tune out for a little bit after that, because I know everything that follows that statement is nothing sincere, but all out of a recited book written by someone who screwed up their own life, and now thousands of people sit around and praise them like they were holy.

"You probably don't understand this, but the program says that we all make mistakes, and it is okay, because you know what?" he asks in a condescending tone.

"What?" I continue in annoyance.

"We can get better, and your mom is getting better."

I look over at her sunken in eyes, grey skin, and overall deathly features."I don't want to hear it from anyone else. You tell me. What are you addicted to?"

"Pot," she grabs my hand, rubbing her cold bony fingers over my warm and sweaty hand, "I am so sorry baby that I didn't tell you. I am going to get help, it is why I'm in the program now."

"You're lying. People can't even get addicted to that," I spit back then look at my grandfather "tell me the truth. Now."

"She's right, Hailey. You need to trust us…" my grandfather starts as I interrupt, "trust? All you guys do is lie. You're lying right now," I cry heavily, gasping in between sobs.

"You need to listen to Pawpaw, he knows what he is talking about," Mom speaks softly, still holding my hand.

I snatch my hand abruptly from her, "How dare you say I don't know what I am talking about." I stand up aggressively, slamming my fist on the table, the chair falling over, "with you," I say as I point to my grandfather, "and you," I continue as I now point at my mother, "and Bobby!" I scream as I run down the stairs.

All three of us know it is a lie. They are both completely aware that I know what is really going on. They just sit there and watch me break into a million pieces, crying profusely running down the stairs, not being able to breathe.

"But uh yeah, it turned out she was highly addicted to cocaine, and whatever else she could get her hands on, and often mixed all of it with alcohol, so ya thats the worst conversation i've

had."

And then I got *that* look.

August 11, 2011

...I have given you your space like you asked me to. But I think it's time to give us a chance...I'm so sorry for everything that has happened. But it was suppose to happen...I pray that you will make a step so we can repair our relationship.

attached testimony letter by sponsor in AA presented to the court, with court stamped approval, that she is fit to be a mother again, for joint custody of Noah.

August 17, 2011

...I sure hope I can see you or at least talk to you before you start the 8th grade.

August 22, 2011

...I hope you have a wonderful first day of school. You are going to have a great school year.

Peanuts

The rain rolls sideways on the window of the car as if each droplet is in a race with the others, and I secretly pull for the least likely victor. Then with the quick turn onto a street or the immediate stop at a light they all crash into each other, and the race is over and I am now bored. I turn towards the road, clueing back into the awful gospel music playing in the car, and my hand reaches for the knob.

"Are you cold?"

"Yeah," I say as I twist the tiny dial towards heat. "So, where are we going to eat again?" I scoot to one side of the tan leathered seat, opposite to the driver, my grandmother.

"Anywhere you want, but first we need to run a quick errand."

Nod.

****

The tan honda makes a turn onto a dirt driveway leading to the back of a church. We come to a complete stop just as the song on the radio comes to an end. Clicking, the emergency brake is pulled up after the car is put in park.

"What are we doing here?" I asked annoyed, but scared to know the answer to the question posed.

"We are worried about you. Pawpaw and I that is."

So you think I need Jesus. My eyes cut hard to my left and I stare through her. Waiting.

"We thought it would be good for you to go to a NA meeting specialized for family members of addicts."

"No, I refuse.'

"Hailey, just give it a try and I promise if you don't like it we won't ever come again."

Rain keeps falling and I think to myself why this is my life, my normal. I watch everyone as they get out of their cars, and head into this stain glassed mecca of uncertainty and lies.

"Are you going with me?"

"No, but I'll be here when you get out, and we can go wherever you want to eat after."

My heart sinks, and I am terrified. I look down at my hands which are aggressively rubbing back and forth on my pants, creating darker shades from the way the fabric is grazed, and I feel my heart start to race.

"I'll walk in with you if you would like."

Nod.

****

We enter the stairwell with papered signs of black arrows and times new roman letters of "NA families this way." I hate this label. I don't want anyone to know this about me. Everyone has secrets, and this is mine.

As we enter the room, it is large. Hospital like lights shine brightly on the tile floor and a large statue of Jesus sits in the corner, staring at me, smiling. Six black chairs are formed in a circle in the far back.

Six.

There is a "snack table" that is labeled consisting of...peanuts. I sit down by a lady who is wearing all black like she is attending her own funeral, with leather skin, bleached blonde hair, and smells of cheap cigarettes. She is the normal one here, and that is sad, because she looks like a commercial for a botox treatment that went wrong, and she was at least 30. The second youngest here, with the first being me. The meeting begins with prayer.

Jesus, I knew it.

We start with introductions, and not all the chairs are full. The middle aged man, the leader so to speak, sitting across from me, and he is too perky. I sit slouched in this cold plastic chair, and I avoid eye contact at all costs.

"Hey Shugah," the leather skin lady speaks, "did you hear that sweetie? We asked your name."

"Oh, umm, Hailey. My name is Hailey." I say as I look around at the circle that surrounds me. The ironic circle that is.

In front of me sits the middle aged man. The leather skin lady beside me, and beside her an old man looking for a little action, either from me or her, but she seems interested. He comes here for ass I can tell by the way he looks at us as if he's seen us naked. The man sitting a chair length distance to my right wears five different shades of brown, and shakes. Did he not get the memo this meeting is for family members of addicts, not addicts themselves?

The leather skin lady speaks first. She complains that her 80 something year old husband no longer has sex with her, no matter the amount of Viagra, and I'm confused as to how the hell this has anything to do with addicts. In fact, she doesn't stop complaining about her life, her unhealthy obsession of shopping, and her frail husband until about 15 minutes until the whole hour meeting is almost over. Finally, the perky middle aged man asks, "And who is the addict you wish to speak of?"

"Oh, that was my dad but he's been dead for years...anyways, these Jimmy Choos.."

I stare at the clock, again not listening to anything being said, and the old man winks at me, and the eyes of the brown dressed man begin to roll back into his head, but then they come back, escaping death once again. Time moves slow, literally, I don't think one of the hands is even moving. Forgiveness and overcoming are written on the board, and I laugh to myself thinking about how textbook this all is. I sit here, staring in silence until I hear, "Well, that concludes our meeting today. In the back are some pamphlets that our statue of Jesus is holding. I encourage you to grab one on your way out. It's information on the dates the meetings are held. Don't forget to grab some snacks on your way out."

Peanuts.

****

I slam the car door as I fling my cold, wet body into the front seat. Gospel still plays on the radio, and my grandmother is reading her dirty pleasure book, out here in the parking lot of the church.

"How was it?"

"Awful, I will never go back again." I spat at her, and break into tears.

"Hailey," she says as she places her clear coated perfectly shaped nails on my shoulder, "we can look into other locations, try new programs."

"No."

"Hailey, this will be good for you."

"You don't know what this is like, or what is good for me, stop pretending like you do. Being the parent to an addict, and the daughter of one is different."

"Hailey…"

"Never. Again."

"Where do you want to eat?" she asks as we begin to pull out.

"I'm not hungry," I say as my stomach growls.

Disconnect

Dad has blocked her number for a year now, but sometimes I call on other people's phones to just hear her voicemail. Her voice, a little hoarse from smoking, a little tired from the night before, but her, a hint of motherliness hidden deep below. Nana slipped up and told me mom was visiting her in Florida where the sun always shines, and where I once enjoyed to visit, but now just reminds me too much of her. Specifically the letter framed hanging in their bathroom, "Dear Mom" it says in my mother's handwriting from an elementary age. Listing all the things that made Nana wonderful, but never existed in my mother. But this doesn't make sense. Mom and her do not talk, not after court dates and picking sides, of rehab clinics, and failed attempts to get her locked up. So I call, because this line isn't blocked. Hello, she picks up, and I hang up, but she calls back, and the ring scares me, and my heart beats, and hello I say. Her voice sounds the same as before, and she tells me she's down there for a visit, but I don't believe her and we both know it. She asks me about school, sports, and boys, but that's not what I want to talk about. So I threaten to hang up, to disconnect our relationship again, and with the panic in her voice, she reveals. A forced abortion, something about some low life guy who hits her and drinks too much and knocked her up. She lost this baby, a miscarriage, and it reminds me of the one she had before me. Of how she constantly reminds me I wasn't her first baby, that her true first child is in Heaven, waiting to meet them, name selected and all. I remember how that baby will always be ranked before me, and I think about how this new one will too. But I'm angry, and confused, and I scream, "How could you get pregnant with another child, when you can't even take care of the ones you already have?"

November 19, 2012

...I haven't been a good mother for years and for that I'm truly sorry. I wish I was the mother I had been for the first half of your life. I'm trying my best to be that mother again...I've had to take a long hard look at myself and I don't like what I see...I will spend all the days of my life making up for the mistakes I have made...I've gotten in such a bad place that it's like I've forgotten how to be a mother. The good thing is, when you do drugs and alcohol, you don't have to feel things, good or bad...Ya'll deserve better because you two are wonderful children. So wonderful, I don't deserve you.

Caramel Apple

The phone rings, a picture of us pops up and 'CamCam Best Mofo In Da World," scrolls across the screen, the only suiting contact name for a friend of this level. Decline. This is the fifth time I have selected the little red button over the green, but something about it seems right. Dark rooms, my dog's snuggles, and Gossip Girl sounds insanely better than hanging out with a lot of people at a place I probably necessarily don't want to be at.

"Hails, let's hang out!" her text reads, way too perky for Cameron.

"I can't…"

"Come on…I haven't seen you in weeks!"

"You see me at school."

"Dude, you know what I mean"

"Ya, but I'm busy right now"

"How long?"

"I don't know."

"Have you eaten?"

"I'm not hungry"

"Hailey…"

"What Cameron? I'm fine okay? You don't have to keep checking up on me. I am just tired and want to rest, go have fun with everyone."

The show ends, and I feel bad for lying about Dad who is actually hours away on a business trip, and I really am hungry, but I don't want to get up, and something about not eating at all sounds a little better than moving. Sleep sounds better than anything, and I...but maybe I should get up.

I open my contacts in my phone, scroll down until I see Dad's name, select "send text" and type "Is it okay if I go out with Camero...but I delete it all and lock my phone. "Play" I press on the screen for the next episode, and I doze in and out of sleep. My hair hasn't been washed in days, and my sweatpants are twisted in with the sheets, but I'm fine.

Serena is off deciding between Nate and Dan, and we all know she'll end up with Dan, and Blair is with Chuck sometimes, and somehow I am with them all. A life created in the made up one of this series, completely absorbed, as hours pass by, and I dwindle. She calls again. Decline, and again.

"Come outside," she texts me as the harsh blue light illuminates the room, and my dog tosses and turns in her sleep, probably dreaming, and I wish my life was as simple as hers. I pretend to be asleep. Lying here, no windows in my room working as an advantage, no way to peer in and catch me in a lie. But then Dori hears the car rumble up the driveway, and she starts barking, first a soft growl, then a ferocious bark for such a small dog. "Shhh…" I whisper to her as if Cameron could hear through these walls, and know I am still breathing, just lying here like a corpse, buried below feet of pillows and blankets.

I think to myself about how long she will have the patience to wait outside until she realizes I am not coming, how many times I can press decline, and how many texts I can screen before she realizes I don't want to see her. Or anyone for that matter. But all I can really think about is how we use to cook chicken nuggets in her microwave after school and dip them in Sweet Baby Ray's

BBQ sauce, and how that reminds me of home with my mother, and how now her home is mine.

How when I walk in, her dogs no longer bark, and I've been told I can come over no matter how late and they won't ask why. I think about jamming to Miley Cyrus' "When I Look at You" with the windows down and chasing sunsets on summer nights. I think about telling her about my first boyfriend, that wasn't her brother, and I think about being in family pictures on her mother's facebook page. I think about all the times I've cried, and laughed, and smiled, and screamed, and all the times I've felt alive.

I creep out of my bed, unlocking my bedroom door, walking up the stairs to peer out and see if she is still there, or if she gave up. I wind the stairs, squeaky at first, then silent as I lift my feet up a little lighter, and tiptoe around the corner. I don't see Betty White, her car we named for its rather old age, so I walk into the kitchen. But then I see her. She sits there. On my back porch, head turned to the yard, and she doesn't even know I'm watching her.

The way her brown hair is swept up in a messy bun, and how she looks relaxed as if she is watching a summer thunderstorm roll in around five. I can leave, I think to myself. She'll never know I am here, but I think of the BBQ sauce, and the photographs, and here I am unlocking the door.

The porch wood boards squeak under their 7 coats of red paint, and the flowers are in full bloom, and the fan above the table and chairs spins round and round, and she's here and so am I. I don't look at her, and she doesn't either. As we both stare into the back yard with the fire pit, patches of grass and those that never grow any, of the rope swing, and my dog running around chasing bees, she slides me a Starbucks cup.

"Caramel Apple," she whispers as she continues looking forward, trying not to disrupt the peace. My pale hand stretches out, grasping it, and sipping the warm sweet liquid, the sun begins to set.

"I love you" and I nod.

Saving Mr. Banks

"Hailey, come on, get up, come upstairs," he knocks softly enough to not upset me, but loud enough to wake me up from my deep slumber. Irritated and lacking energy, I roll out of my white crinkled duvet, and turn off the fan that blows around dust and dead skin particles. I unlock the door, but dare not to turn on the light, leaving my dark den of no windowed bedroom, and chilling atmosphere to the house of colors and loud music playing.

"What?" I ask annoyed as I approach the island in the kitchen, where dad stands cooking dinner, the overwhelming smell of garlic taking over the room. I see it in his dark brown eyes that something is different. He is gentle, not hard and grey hair, but concerned. I prop up against the couch, staring at my feet. It is just us, and our dog, but it feels crowded. "What are your plans tonight?" he asks me a little too cheery.

"Nothing, probably just staying here, maybe go to bed early, watch a little tv," I continue, still staring down. "What's Grant up to?" he says as he stirs the pasta, tomatoes, and chicken in the pot that sends steam to the ceiling, and I hope for the fire alarm to go off to end this conversation.

"I don't know, why?"

"He's your boyfriend, and it is a Friday night."

"Okay? But I don't want to."

"You haven't been out in weeks, all you do is sleep."

"I'm tired!" I scream defensively.

"I want you to call him," he stares at me firmly, one eyebrow raised, a single hair sticking out a little longer than the rest from a dream the previous night.

"I don't want to. Why can't we just hang out?" tears beginning to swelter in my eyes.

He looks at me, bald head, kind of resembling a younger, more life-like version of Mr. Clean, beard a little grey and white, worn out and warm, sipping on his glass of wine. "Call."

I roll my eyes, pick up my phone, scrolling to recents, finger hesitating over the call button, and I stare at him blue eyed and teary. Call.

A few hours later, and we sit here. Grant and I, in a theatre filled of children, loud chomping of popcorn, and an excessive amount of Twizzlers. The previews have just started and he tries to touch me, but I don't want to be touched. I don't want questions of why I haven't returned his calls, or locked myself in my room, or why Cameron, my absolute best friend, showed up to check on me and how everyone knows I wouldn't answer the door. I don't want these questions because I know it means he sees me differently, and I am her. Depressed and mentally ill, broken and fragile in the eyes of many, a carbon copy of my mother.

Eyes forward, I watch the opening of Disney's, <u>Saving Mr. Banks</u> the title says. I think to myself Disney is for children, and there is comfort in that. As the movie progresses, I shift a little closer, head on his shoulder, thinking this is what people do. Now there is a scene of Mary Poppins, the real one. The one who acted like a mother, who came and went, and no one knows where she is, or how she's doing. How the children needed her. Their father, addicted to a liquid that made him absent. They beg. Beg for attention, love, care, the return of a parent, and they cry. I cry.

A little tear, rolling down my face, and I can taste its saltiness as it meets my lips. I sit back up, reclusing back into the darkness of the theatre, but the tears increase, and now there is a hand on my knee and I don't want it to be. I don't want to think of her, or be her, or...or...and I cry. His arms around me, and I just want my darkness, my bed, and my loneliness.

We sit in the car, crying, well I cry, and Grant stares forward. The car is fogging up from hot breath, but not the kind most teenagers experience. Rather, the ones that come from gasps for air, and "I miss her" talks, and "it's been years." We sit here and Grant doesn't know what to do with me.

"Save me," I whisper.

Drops of Jupiter

We drive in the dark, and we are the only car left on the road, or any road for that matter. The stop light moves from yellow, to red, to green, and no one comes. The trees look like silhouettes of scary stick men lurking in the shadows. The wind whistling through the branches, leaves shaking. The black car blends in with the streets which further blends into the outside and all its darkness. She swerves in and out of the white paint, and the baby cries in the back seat. The only light comes from fog lights, and the small flame coming from her lighter. Her hands shake, and the steering wheel shifts. We drift. "God dammit, Hailey! Grab the steering wheel! Can't you see I am busy doing something? Yes, yes, keep it steady." Her knee balances the other side, and my pale skin reflects upon the light of the cigarette. I try to keep the beat up leather steering wheel steady but only guessing as to what that really means. I am too short to see over the wheel. *Straight. Straight.* I think.

"Mom! I can't do this, mom!" I scream at her because I am scared, and my breathing increases, and the baby screams because we scream. "Stop smoking, please! Dad said in your papers it says you aren't allowed to smoke in the car with me because of my asthma!"

"The window is down! You are fine!"

"Barely! Mom put your hands back, please! Mom!"

He screams, and cries louder.

"Shut up! Shut up!" she screams with her hands covering her ears, eyes closed, still behind the steering wheel, ash dropping on her leg.

"Mom, put out the cigarette. Grab the steering wheel!"

"I am your mother! You don't get to tell me what I do and don't get to do," she spats as she throw my hands off the wheel, her cigarette dangling out of her mouth, and brushing the ash off her leg with her other hand.

"Dad said you aren't allowed to smoke with me," I say as I begin to cough and breathe heavier.

"Is your dad here? No. So stop bringing him up. You are like his little spy, he doesn't need to know everything that is going on here." The car keeps swerving, but I see headlights. Headlights that indicate we aren't alone.

"I'm just saying…"

"You're always "just saying," she mocks me.

"I wish I was with Dad…" I say under my breath.

"What did you say to me? You wish you were with your dad huh?"

I sit silently scared to look over to see the face of the monster she has become. Even the crying in the back stopped as if he knew just as I did that something was about to come of this. And whatever it was it was nothing but bad.

She continues, "I know you think your dad is all high and mighty, but he isn't. He isn't everything you think he is, your prince charming? Your savior? From what, me? Ha!" she starts laughing a creepy, eerie laugh, as if she is a villain in her own tv show.

"Mom, stop. Please, I don't like when you just talk bad about him. He doesn't do it to you."

"Of course he doesn't," as if my statement just proved every idiotic thought she just had.

"I just don't like it, mom." I stare out of the window, completely angling my body to face the outside, as if only my body is in the car, but mind and soul are gone from the toxic environment within.

"You know what, your dad," she starts as she throws the bud of the cigarette out of the window, finally, "your dad does wrong too. He use to…"

I put my hands over my ears now, roles reversing. "Shut up! Shut up!"

She takes one hand off the steering wheel, pulling at my hands attached to my ears, screaming a muffled scream, "You listen to me dammit!"

I take my hands off my ears, look at her and she continues, "You know he use to abuse me!"

"Shut up!"

Before I could even comprehend what just occurred, my hand resting on my face, the blood rushing to my cheeks, followed by a quick stinging sensation, and a single tear running down it like an ice cube to a fire.

"I'm so sorry baby, I am sorry. I don't know what I was thinking, I didn't mean to hit you."

I pull away, inching as far as I could to the opposite side of the car. Drops of Jupiter begins playing on the radio.

****

It's Halloween, and all the houses in the neighborhood are decorated with ghouls, goblins, and skeletons, but not mine. Mine consists of the same dead flowers in overgrown flower beds, accompanied by overgrown grass. Mine consists of no lights, or decorations, or eerie music. Not even a pumpkin. The neighbors always drop off cookies and treats, for the kids, but they are rationed off by our parents. This year they dropped off a pumpkin, a little one that is supposed to decorate a kitchen table or windowsill. As I sit around and see all the decorations, I think of what it must be like to be those kinds of families. I wish I had a mom who did my makeup and dressed me up for halloween, but where is my mom? Missing, per usual. I'll be right back she says, but I have heard this before. So instead, I choose to decorate the pumpkin and put it on the porch.

I pull my orange wavy hair up in a ponytail, making sure there are not bumps, patting it down and smoothing it out. I look at the pumpkin, at its ridges and curves. Its bruises and hard spots, and the way its stem was cut off so abruptly. I want to carve it, but I don't like the way the seeds and "guts" feel. Also, I am scared to cut myself, but mainly because the guts remind me of throw up, so I pull out my drawer of markers, pulling out the best ones, the cutest and darkest colors. Then I pull out the other drawers, gathering together any stickers, or anything that can make this pumpkin worthy of the front stoop. I uncap the crayola dark blue marker and begin to write: *Tell me did you sail across the sun, did you make it to the Milky Way to see the lights all faded and that heaven is overrated.*

****

"Hand me that box, sweetie," Mom says as she closes up another one with some clear squeaky packers tape and a black sharpie.

She keeps trying to cheer me up and convince me that this move is an "exciting new start for our family" but I see the foreclosure sign in the front yard. It sways back and forth, and I know why it's there. It has nothing to do with a new start, or an upgrade or downgrade, but rather a nasty habit that robbed my money, my family's, and my child support. The longer we stand in the garage, the more the brown cardboard grows and items disappear, and fake smiles keep reappearing, the less I want to be here. "Honey, did you hear me?"

"What?" I say as I pull the earbud out of my ear, pausing Drops of Jupiter on my iPod.

"Hand me that box please."

****

The thunder roars, shaking the figurines decorated on my white furniture, and lightning lights up the room. I see myself in flashes. I lie under blankets, covering my body like a newborn baby swaddled, comfortable with confined movement. I am not afraid of the storm outside, but rather the storm inside. The thunder that knocks heavily on my door, and the screams that strike the doorway like the lightning bolts that occur outside. The door handle keeps shaking, and I pray that it holds up, never giving way to the disaster that remains outside. I hum to myself my favorite song, that comforts me from the craziness. *Now that she's back in the atmosphere, with drops of jupiter in her hair, hey, hey.*

****

It is hot, 95 but it feels like 100, and we are sweaty. We stand on blankets, and dance hoping that a breeze will go up our skirts because we are so hot. Tonight I am young, and I am with my friends. We are sober, but it feels like we are drunk because we are in the moment and we are happy. The sun has set, but it still feels like the sun is shining. The people dance, and they kiss, and the amphitheatre is filled. We are in the lawn section because we can't afford close up seats, but it's okay because we are together, and we dance to some of our favorite music. The encore is my favorite song, Drops of Jupiter, and I have waited all night for it. But it is different, and I realize that as soon as the music starts. I look around and everyone seems normal. Their eyes look forward, their hips move in rhythm, and they sing. But I, I notice something different. It isn't the air, or the people that surround me, or the way the song it is performed. It is me. It is the first time I realized now when I hear the song, I am no longer the girl looking for herself out there, or wishing I was in space instead of here, but rather I am me, and I am happy. It isn't an escape song, but it is now a song I just have long enjoyed. Something within me changes, and I cry. A little peaceful cry, with a smile, and I feel a hand grasp mine, then two others. Finally, we are all holding hands, and we scream to the skies: *AND THE DROPS OF JUPITER IN HER HAIR.*

June 1, 2014-

Hey there my sweet angel. Remember when I always called you that when you were little? I absolutely loved my pictures and letter. You have no idea how much it meant to me. Words can't even express. I'm so glad you told me everything you have been doing...you wear contacts now? It's funny, it took me so long to get use to you in glasses. You look so different now, but no matter what you always look beautiful...I was in the shower the other day and I just started sobbing...I told God I was ready to be a mother again.

About the Artist

Nicole who was born in 1997 is on the brink of her career. She is currently attending Savannah College of Art and Design focusing in the arts, specifically painting. The artist and illustrator grew up together, attending schooling leading up to their high school graduation, and furthering their friendship through college as well. They chose to do this collaboration to not only promote the other, but support one another as well. Nicole is highly dedicated to her work, and has been featured in galleries, contests, and even her pieces have been bought in auctions. Both author and illustrator are from Greensboro, North Carolina, but reside out of state for schooling. Always remember to support the arts, and your local artists too.

Made in the USA
Middletown, DE
26 June 2017